Collins
French Club

FUN, ACTIVE LEARNING

Book 1

Rosi McNab

First published in 2009 by Collins
an imprint of HarperCollins Publishers
77–85 Fulham Palace Road
London w6 8jb

www.collinslanguage.com

9 8 7 6 5 4 3 2 1 0

A catalogue record for this book is available
from the British Library

Author: Rosi McNab
Illustrator: Mel Sharp
Designer: Rob Payne

ISBN: 978-0-00-784004-5

This edition produced for The Book People Ltd,
Park Menai, Bangor, LL57 4FB

CD recording by Talking Issues
Music by Myra Barretto and Daniel Murguialday
Actors: Claudia Jenkins, Samuel Jenkins, Laurène
Lebrat and Kevin Lebrat
Printed in China through
Golden Cup Printing Services

Contents

1

AU ZOO

1. At the zoo

Help your child: Most French words for animals look like the English but sound quite different. This unit is about learning how to pronounce these words in the French way. Have fun listening to the CD with your child and try to copy the pronunciation.

Allons au zoo!
Let's go to the zoo!

Chanson: Écoute et chante
Song: Listen and sing

Track 1

Je suis allé(e) au zoo et j'ai vu …
I went to the zoo and I saw

Qu'as-tu vu?
What did you see?

J'ai vu … un kangourou!
I saw … a kangaroo!

Un kangourou? C'est tout?
A kangaroo? Is that all?

Oui, c'est tout.
Yes, that's all.

Je suis allé(e) au zoo et j'ai vu …
Qu'as-tu vu?
J'ai vu … un kangourou et une girafe!
Un kangourou et une girafe? C'est tout?
Oui, c'est tout.

Je suis allé(e) …

UN KANGOUROU

UNE GIRAFE

UN CHIMPANZÉ

UN LION

UN ÉLÉPHANT

UN CROCODILE

Écoute le CD, puis colle les vignettes au bon endroit
Listen to the CD, then stick the stickers in the right places

Track 2

T I P

Astuce
Where do I start?!
Do the easy ones first and see what you have left!

KANGOUROU

CHIMPANZÉ

CROCODILE

LION

TIGRE

GIRAFE

HIPPOPOTAME

ÉLÉPHANT

TORTUE

Astuce
A lot of French words look the same as English but they don't sound the same. Try to say them in the French way.

Au zoo 3

Complète les mots et relie les mots à la bonne image
Complete the words and join the words to the right pictures

le c .r. o .c. odile

le k ..... ng .... rou

le l .... n

l' ..... i .... o ..... otame

la g ..... ra ..... e

le t .... re

l'élé .... nt

Astuce
If a French word begins with an *h* like *hippopotame*, the *h* is silent.

Le détective!
Did you notice?

Je suis un **ch**ampion!

A lot of French words look like English words but they are said in a different way. Find a French word with *ch* in it and use the CD to work out how it is pronounced.

Which is true? Underline the correct answer:

In French, *ch* sounds like ...

1. *ch* in *chair*   2. *sh* in *shoe*

Now try saying these *ch* words aloud:

champignon
mushroom

chien
dog

cheval
horse

château
castle

chenille
caterpillar

ch

4 **Au zoo**

Mots cachés: Combien d'animaux peux-tu trouver?
Word search: How many animals can you find?

m	e	r	s	t	i	g	r	e
c	r	o	c	o	d	i	l	e
k	a	n	g	o	u	r	o	u
l	é	l	é	p	h	a	n	t
f	i	i	g	q	v	f	n	l
t	t	o	r	t	u	e	é	s
b	j	n	é	d	c	l	g	é

Le détective!
Did you notice?

Some letters have accents on them. This accent ´ is called an acute accent or, in French, an *accent aigu.* It changes the way the letter sounds. Find a French word with *é* in it and use the CD to work out how it is pronounced.

Which is true? Underline the correct answer:

In French, é sounds like ...

1. *e* as in *egg*   2. *ay* as in *day*   3. *ea* as in *tea*

Now try saying these *é* words aloud:

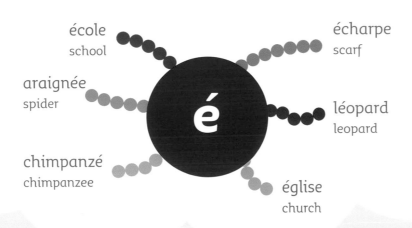

école
school

écharpe
scarf

araignée
spider

é

léopard
leopard

chimpanzé
chimpanzee

église
church

Au zoo 5

Combien?

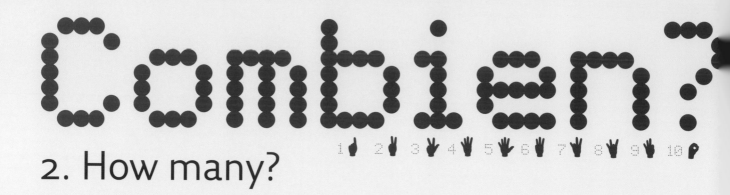

2. How many?

Help your child: French words are often not pronounced as they look. Encourage your child to concentrate on the sounds of the words; the spelling will come later. Languages are all about communication – so the first step is to get talking.

Rime: Écoute et participe
Rhyme: Listen and join in

Track 3

o zéro

1 un

2 deux

3 trois

4 quatre

5 cinq

6 six

7 sept

8 huit

9 neuf

10 dix

un éléphant
deux dauphins
trois tortues
quatre queues
cinq singes
six cerfs
sept serpents
huit chenilles
neuf nids
dix dinosaures

Colle les vignettes au bon endroit
Stick the stickers in the right places

Le détective!
Did you notice?

A lot of French words aren't pronounced quite as you might imagine.

Which is true? Underline the correct answer:

1. *Deux* sounds like a) duck b) duh c) do
2. *Quatre* sounds like a) cat b) quad c) quit
3. *Cinq* sounds like a) sink b) chink c) sank
4. *Huit* begins like a) *whe* as in wheel b) *hu* as in hum c) *hoo* as in hoof
5. *Neuf* begins like a) *ne* as in new b) *nev* as in never c) *nur* as in nurse
6. *Dix* begins like a) *di* as in dice b) *de* as in December c) *di* as in dirty

Chanson: Écoute et chante
Song: Listen and sing

Track 4

Un éléphant qui se balançait
An elephant who was swinging

Sur une toile d'araignée
On a spider's web

Trouva ce jeu si amusant
He found this game so amusing

Qu'il alla chercher un autre éléphant.
He went to find another elephant.

Deux éléphants qui se balançaient ...

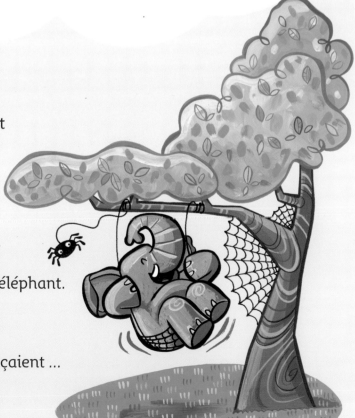

Combien? 7

Complète les dessins
Complete the drawings

quatre ballons

trois chenilles

deux papillons

cinq araignées

sept souris

Dessine des os pour relier les mots et les images et écris les lettres qui manquent
Draw bones (os) linking the words and the pictures and fill in the missing letters

D .... x os

H .... t os

S .... t os

Petit Dico

os bone(s)

Qu .... e os

Tr .... s os

N .... f os

Entoure les chiffres
Put a ring around the numbers in each list

chien, chenille, cinq, chat

deux, dessin, disque, dix

singe, sept, souris, six

question, queue, quatre, qui

fruit, huit, nuit, bruit

trois, bois, fois, mois

Astuce
There are words here that you don't yet know. Why not look them up in a French dictionary?

8 Combien?

Quel âge as-tu?
How old are you?

Dessine les bougies sur les gâteaux
Draw the candles onto the cakes

Comment tu t'appelles?
What are you called?

Quel âge as-tu?
How old are you?

Je m'appelle Hugo
I am called Hugo

J'ai neuf ans
I am nine (years old)

Je m'appelle Manon

J'ai trois ans

Je m'appelle Luc
J'ai sept ans

Je m'appelle Stéphanie

J'ai huit ans

Je m'appelle Sophie
J'ai six ans

Je m'appelle Pierre

J'ai dix ans

Et toi?
And you?

Comment tu t'appelles?

Je ....

Quel âge as-tu?

....

Dessine les bougies sur ton gâteau
Draw some candles on your cake

Coloriage

3. Colouring in

Help your child: This unit introduces the vocabulary for colours. In French, colours have to agree in number and gender with the thing they describe. Don't worry too much about the spelling for now. Build your child's confidence in their spoken French and they will soon be able to transfer this to all other aspects of the language.

Écoute et participe
Listen and join in

 Track 5

 ROUGE

 BLEU

 VERT

JAUNE

 MARRON

BLANC

 NOIR

 GRIS

 ROSE

 VIOLET

 ORANGE

Colorie les chapeaux
Colour in the hats

un chapeau jaune et rose

un chapeau bleu et rouge

une casquette rouge et grise

un chapeau vert et marron

un chapeau noir et orange

un béret violet et bleu

10 Coloriage

Colle le bon cerf-volant au bon endroit
Stick the right kites in the right places

CLARA　　THOMAS　　HUGO　　STÉPHANIE　　ZOÉ　　LOUIS

Clara: "Mon cerf-volant est rouge et jaune"

Le cerf-volant d'Hugo est blanc et noir

Le cerf-volant de Zoé est bleu et jaune

Thomas a un cerf-volant bleu et vert

Stéphanie a un cerf-volant rose et gris

Louis: "Mon cerf-volant est vert et rouge"

Dessine un cerf-volant et colorie-le
Draw a kite and colour it in

Complète la phrase
Complete the sentence

Mon cerf-volant est .... et ....

Coloriage 11

Colorie les images
Colour in the pictures

un ballon rouge

un oiseau jaune

un papillon bleu

une souris grise

un gâteau marron

une chenille verte

un éléphant gris

un chien noir

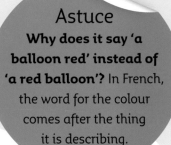

Astuce
Why does it say 'a balloon red' instead of 'a red balloon'? In French, the word for the colour comes after the thing it is describing.

Le détective!
Did you notice?

Some of the words for colours add an -e if the thing they are describing is a feminine word. You'll learn more about masculine and feminine words in Unit 5 but for now, remember that if a word has *une* before it rather than *un*, the colour will likely need an -e on the end.

un papillon bleu   but   une fleur bleue
a blue butterfly   a blue flower

un chapeau vert   but   une chenille verte
a green hat   a green caterpillar

Some words for colours already end in -e (rouge/jaune/orange) so they don't change. Put a ring around the two colours in the exercise above which have **added** an -e.

12 **Coloriage**

L'arc en ciel
The rainbow

Écoute et participe, puis colorie l'arc en ciel
Listen and join in, then colour in the rainbow

Track 6

ROUGE ORANGE JAUNE VERT BLEU VIOLET ROSE

Écris un poème
Write a poem

If you can't think of any French words to use, why not go onto the internet? At www.collinslanguage.com there is a dictionary to help you. You can type in an English word and it will tell you how you spell it in French! Or you can use the words in the *petit dico* below.

Astuce
Do I have to add an -e to some colours in my poem? No. The ending only changes when it comes straight after the word it is describing: *bleu comme la mer* but *la mer bleue.*

Noir comme   *la nuit* ....

Blanc comme   ....

Rouge comme   ....

Gris comme   ....

Jaune comme   ....

Vert comme   ....

Petit Dico
la nuit the night
le soleil the sun
la neige the snow
la mer the sea
une feuille a leaf
une tomate a tomato
un éléphant an elephant

Coloriage 13

Tu Es Comment?

4. What do you look like?

Help your child: This unit concentrates on how to describe people. This will help to reinforce colours vocabulary whilst introducing new words like 'long', 'short', 'blonde' and 'glasses'. Encourage your child to use this new vocabulary to describe people in family photos.

Colorie les cheveux et les yeux
Colour the hair and eyes

SOPHIE

J'ai les cheveux noirs et les yeux bruns

MARC

J'ai les cheveux bruns et les yeux verts

MARIE

J'ai les yeux bleus et les cheveux bruns

PHILIPPE

J'ai les yeux bruns et les cheveux noirs

RICHARD

J'ai les cheveux roux et les yeux noisettes

NADINE

J'ai les cheveux blonds et les yeux bleus

Et toi?

Moi? J'ai les ....

et les ....

Qui est-ce?
Who is it?

THOMAS

CLARA

STEPHANIE

ZOÉ

LOUIS

HUGO

1. J'ai les cheveux mi-longs, frisés et bruns:

....

2. J'ai les cheveux courts, noirs et frisés:

....

3. Mes cheveux sont noirs, blonds et courts:

....

4. Mes cheveux sont bruns et courts:

....

5. Mes cheveux sont raides et blonds:

....

6. J'ai les cheveux longs, raides et noirs et je porte des lunettes:

....

Petit Dico

les cheveux hair
les yeux eyes
longs long
mi-longs shoulder-length
courts short
frisés curly
raides straight

roux red/ginger
noisette hazel/green-brown
blond blonde
brun brown
Je porte I wear
les lunettes glasses

Tu es comment? 15

Petite histoire: La famille des caméléons

A little story: The chameleon family

Écoute et lis. Puis, colle le bon caméléon au bon endroit
Listen and read. Then, stick the right chameleon in the right places

Track 7

Je suis Monsieur Caméléon.
I am Mr Chameleon.

J'habite dans un arbre.
I live in a tree.

Je mange des insectes.
I eat insects.

Regarde! Je suis vert comme une feuille.
Look, I'm green like a leaf.

Je suis Madame Caméléon.
I am Mrs Chameleon.

J'adore les fleurs.
I love flowers.

Oh, quelle jolie fleur rose!
Oh, what a pretty pink flower!

Regarde, je suis rose comme une fleur!
Look, I'm pink like a flower!

Je suis Chloé Caméléon.
I am Chloe Chameleon.

J'adore les papillons.
I love butterflies.

Oh, quel joli papillon jaune!
Oh, what a pretty yellow butterfly!

Regarde, je suis jaune comme le papillon!
Look, I'm yellow like the butterfly!

Petit Dico

un arbre tree
Je mange I eat
Regarde! Look!
Je suis I am
comme like
joli(e) nice/pretty
camouflé camouflaged
une sauterelle a grasshopper
Et toi? And you?
J'adore I love
délicieux/euse delicious

16 Tu es comment?

Je m'appelle Camille Caméléon.
My name is Camille Chameleon.

J'adore les fleurs.
I love flowers.

J'adore les jolies jacinthes bleues.
I love blue hyacinths.

Oh là là, je suis toute bleue comme les fleurs!
Wow, I am completely blue like the flowers!

Je m'appelle Christian Caméléon.
My name is Christian Chameleon.

Je suis camouflé.
I am camouflaged.

Je me cache.
I'm hiding.

Ah regarde, une sauterelle … ah bon, le dîner.
Oh look, a grasshopper … mmmm, dinner.

J'adore les sauterelles.
I love grasshoppers.

Elles sont délicieuses.
They are delicious.

Et toi? Tu manges des sauterelles?
And you? Do you eat grasshoppers?

Colorie le caméléon et complète la phrase
Colour in your own chameleon and complete the sentence

Mon caméléon est .... comme ....

5. Le or la?

Help your child: All nouns in French are either masculine or feminine. Learning each new word with its *le* or *la* will pay off later on. Try introducing your child to image association – 'mouse' takes the feminine *la* so draw a mouse in a pretty skirt. Using lots of colour will aid memorisation.

All words in French are *le* or *la* words.

le words are masculine words (m) and *la* words are feminine words (f)

Entoure les mots masculins en bleu et les mots féminins en rose
Put a blue ring round the *le* words and a pink ring round the *la* words

le parapluie   le papillon   la chenille   la tortue   le lapin

la fleur   la grenouille   le chien   la souris   le ballon

Choisis des mots et écris-les sur ta toile
Choose some words to write on your own word web

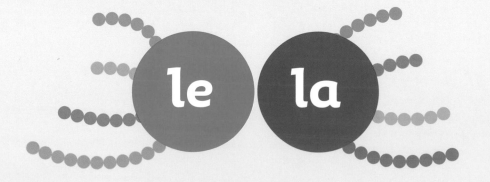

le   la

Dessine ou colle des images dans les cases
Draw or stick some pictures into the boxes

MASCULINE WORDS

Astuce
Does it matter if I don't get the *le* and *la* right? You will still be understood if you make mistakes, but it helps a lot later on if you learn new words with their *le* and *la*. French children have to!

FEMININE WORDS

Le détective!
Did you notice?

If a French word begins with a vowel (a, e, i, o, u) like *éléphant*, or an *h* like *hippopotame*, you use *l'* instead of *le* or *la* because it makes it easier to say.

Try it! (Remember not to pronounce the *h*)

le hippopotame or l'hippopotame

Which do you find easier to say?

Complète le texte avec *le*, *la* ou *l'*
Write *le*, *la* or *l'* in the spaces

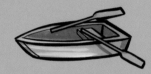

.... bateau (m)

.... chapeau (m)

.... oiseau (m)

.... soleil (m)

.... feuille (f)

.... maison (f)

.... pomme (f)

.... escargot (m)

.... arbre (m)

.... écureuil (m)

.... château (m)

.... hélicoptère (m)

.... hôtel (m)

.... hippopotame (m)

.... école (f)

20 Le ou la?

AU CIRQUE

PRIX DES BILLETS
Adulte €25
Enfant (2-12 ans) €12
Étudiant et personne âgée €18

6. At the circus

Help your child: In this unit the words for 'a' are introduced, continuing your child's study of word gender. The circus theme introduces lots of fun new vocabulary. Try listening to the CD without the book at first to encourage your child to understand as much as possible without the aid of a translation.

Mots qui riment: Écoute et participe
Words that rhyme: Listen and join in

Track 8

Un ballon et une bille,
A ball and a marble,

Un garçon et une fille.
A boy and a girl.

Un frère et une sœur,
A brother and a sister,

Un jardin et une fleur.
A garden and a flower.

Un pain et une baguette,
A loaf and a baguette,

Un vélo et une trottinette.
A bike and a scooter.

Un citron et une prune,
A lemon and a plum,

Un jongleur et un clown.
A juggler and a clown.

Un sac et une trousse,
A bag and a pencil case,

Un dessert et une mousse,
A dessert and a mousse,

Une mousse au chocolat,
A chocolate mousse,

Miam miam!
Yum yum!

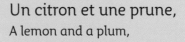

Le clown mange une prune!
The clown eats a plum!

Le détective!
Did you notice?

In the rhyme on the previous page, there was an *un* or an *une* before all of the nouns. *Un* and *une* both mean 'a'.
You use *un* with masculine words and *une* with feminine words.
All *le* words are *un* words and all *la* words are *une* words.

le chien   la trottinette
un chien   une trottinette

Easy!

Écris *un* ou *une* dans les blancs
Write *un* or *une* in each space

 .... parapluie (le parapluie)

 .... fleur (la fleur)

 .... clown (le clown)

 .... veste (la veste)

 .... chaussure (la chaussure)

 .... chapeau (le chapeau)

 .... cravate (la cravate)

 .... chemise (la chemise)

Colorie l'image et complète le texte avec *un* ou *une*
Colour the picture and complete the text with *un* ou *une*

Le clown porte .... pantalon, ... veste,

.... chemise, ... cravate, ... chapeau,

.... fleur, ... parapluie et deux enormes chaussures.

Relie les noms aux images
Link the names to the pictures

Monsieur Loyal

le clown

le jongleur

le cavalier

le trapéziste

la funambule

Au cirque 23

MES VÊTEMENTS

7. My clothes

Help your child: The focus in this unit is on clothing, and consolidates use of gender and colours. Using family photos, you can encourage extra practice. If an item of clothing is not mentioned in the book, help your child to look up the word in a dictionary or online at www.collinslanguage.com.

Qu'est-ce que tu mets?
What are you wearing?

Colorie les vêtements et complète les descriptions
Colour in the clothes and complete the descriptions

 une robe rose

 un jean ....

 un t-shirt jaune

 un pantalon gris

 une chemise bleue

 un sweat ....

 un jogging bleu

 un short ....

 un maillot de bain rouge

 un pyjama ....

 un maillot de foot ....

 une jupe noire

Colorie les chaussures et complète les descriptions
Colour in the shoes and complete the descriptions

 des baskets rouges

 des chaussures ....s

 des tennis ....s

 des pantoufles roses

 des bottes marron

 des palmes ....s

 des bottes de caoutchou ....s

Le détective!
Did you notice?

All of the shoes have the word *des* before them. *Des* means 'some'. In French you say:

je porte des chaussettes   I wear some socks

It doesn't matter if the word is masculine or feminine – if there is more than one thing, you can use *des*.

un ....
une .... des

Colle les vignettes au bon endroit
Stick the stickers in the right place

Je joue au basket

Je vais à l'école

Il pleut

Il neige

Je vais au lit

Je vais faire de la plongée

Qu'est-ce que je mets?

What am I wearing?

Colorie les dessins et remplis les blancs

Colour and label the pictures

Je mets mon jean bleu, mon sweat violet et mes baskets rouges.

....

mon jean bleu ....

....

ZOÉ

Je mets mon maillot de foot rouge, mon short orange et mes chaussures de foot noires.

....

....

....

HUGO

Je mets ma robe verte, mon chapeau jaune et les chaussures de maman.

....

....

....

STÉPHANIE

Je mets mon pantalon noir, mon tee-shirt rouge et mes baskets noires.

....

....

....

THOMAS

26 Mes vêtements

Relie les mots en français aux mots en anglais
Join the French and English words

des baskets	shirt
une chemise	T-shirt
un jean	skirt
un jogging	tracksuit
une jupe	dress
un maillot de foot	swimming costume
un maillot de bain	pyjamas
un pantalon	trousers
un pyjama	football shirt
une robe	jeans
un short	sweatshirt
un sweat	trainers
un tee-shirt	shorts

Astuce
There are so many new words! Where do I start?
Well, lots of them are very like English. Do the ones you can guess first and then see what you have left.

Dessine des vêtements et écris les mots
Draw some clothes and write the words

Je porte...

Les jours de la semaine

The days of the week

lundi
Monday

mardi
Tuesday

mercredi
Wednesday

jeudi
Thursday

vendredi
Friday

samedi
Saturday

dimanche
Sunday

Devinette: Complète la grille pour trouver un nouveau mot de haut en bas

Word puzzle: Fill in the grid to find a new word in the vertical column

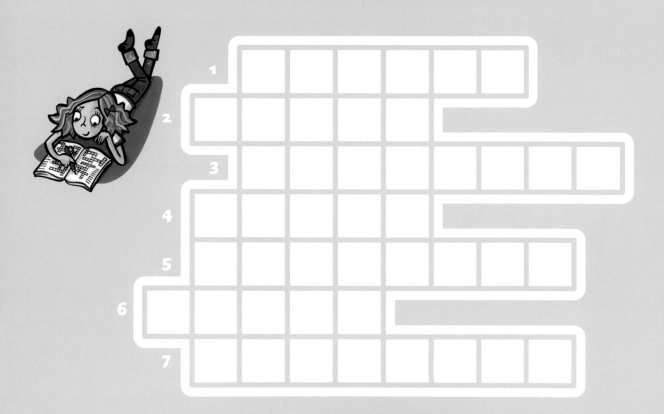

1. The first day of the weekend

2. The day that begins with a *j*

3. The day after *mardi*

4. The day after *lundi*

5. The only day that doesn't end in *di*

6. The first day of the school week

7. The day after *jeudi*

The word that is spelled out is: ....

28 Mes vêtements

Comptine: Écoute et chante

A little ditty: Listen and sing

Track 9

lundi je fais de la musique
on Monday I have music

mardi je fais de la gymnastique
on Tuesday I do gymnastics

mercredi je reste au lit
on Wednesday I stay in bed

jeudi je mange à la cantine
on Thursday I eat in the canteen

vendredi je chante une comptine
on Friday I sing a ditty

et samedi et dimanche ... c'est les vacances!
and on Saturday and Sunday ... we're on holiday!

Le détective!

Did you notice?

The song says *mercredi je reste au lit.* This is because in France it's very common for there to be no school on Wednesdays. French kids are lucky!

Où?

8. Where?

Help your child: This unit introduces prepositions using everyday vocabulary. Encourage your child to try to use this new vocabulary when you are doing other things together. Remember to indulge your child's curiosity by looking up new words in the dictionary or online at www.collinslanguage.com.

Dans, sur, sous
In, on, under

LE CHAT EST SUR LE LIT

LE CHIEN EST DANS LE LIT

LE DINOSAURE EST SOUS LE LIT

Écris le mots qui manquent et colle les vignettes au bon endroit
Write in the missing words and stick the stickers in the correct places

Je me cache .... la table

Je saute .... le trampoline

Je dors .... mon lit

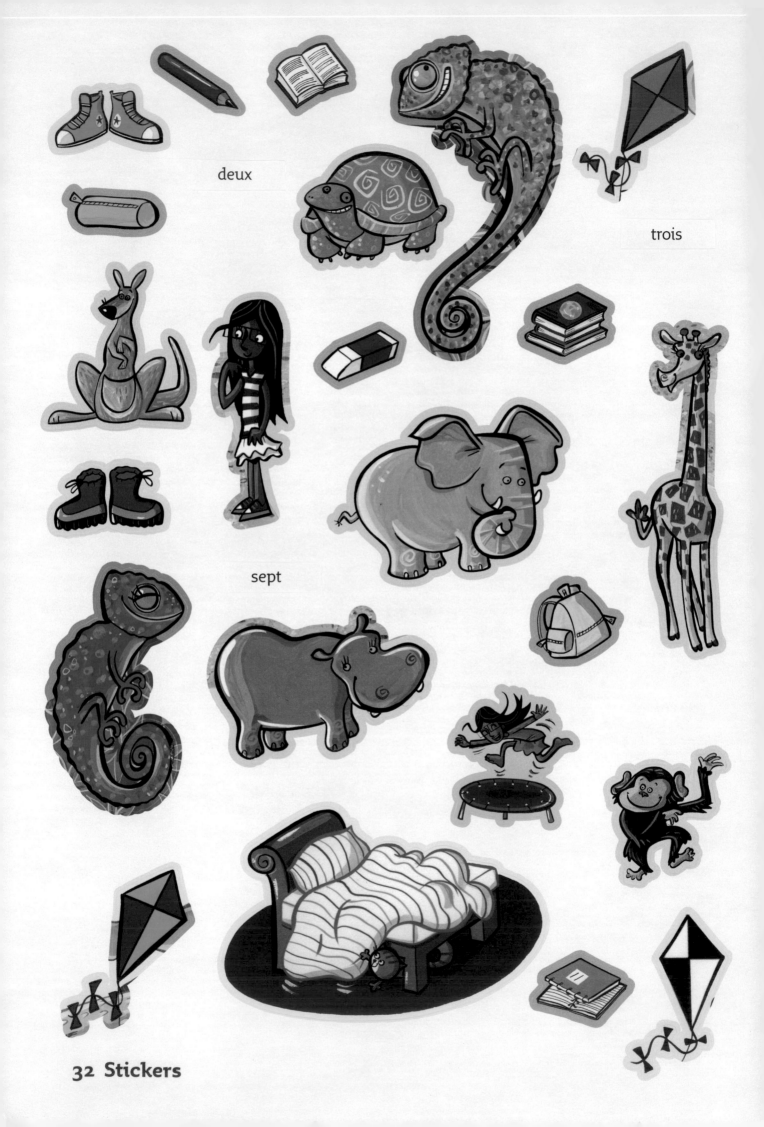

deux

trois

sept

32 Stickers

Écoute le poème
Listen to the poem

Track 10

Dans la forêt il y a un arbre.
In the forest there is a tree.

Un arbre?
A tree?

Oui, un arbre. Et dans l'arbre il y a une branche.
Yes, a tree. And in the tree there is branch.

Une branche?
A branch?

Oui, une branche. Et sur la branche il y a un nid.
Yes, a branch. And on the branch there is a nest.

Un nid?
A nest?

Oui, un nid. Et dans le nid il y a un œuf.
Yes, a nest. And in the nest there is an egg.

Un œuf?
An egg?

Oui, un œuf. Et dans l'œuf il y a …
Yes, an egg. And in the egg there is …

Qu'est-ce qu'il y a?
What is there?

Il y a un petit oiseau.
There is a small bird.

Qu'il est mignon!
It's so sweet!

Où? 35

Colorie les dessins et remplis les blancs

Colour the drawings and complete the sentences

La souris est ...

.... le chapeau

.... le chapeau

.... le chapeau

Le gâteau est ...

.... la table

.... la table

.... l'estomac du chien!

Le détective!

Did you notice?

There was a new accent in the word for 'cake'? It was ∧.

It is called a circumflex accent or *un accent circonflexe*.

It can be put on top of any vowel (a, e, i, o, u).

It doesn't change the sound of the letter but it often goes where there is an *s* in English. Like this:

â as in *les pâtes* (p**as**ta)   ê as in *la forêt* (for**es**t)

î as in *l'île* (**is**le or **is**land)   ô as in *l'hôpital* (h**os**pital)

û as in *août* (Aug**us**t)

Chanson: Écoute et chante. Puis, colle le chaton au bon endroit

Song: Listen and sing. Then, stick the stickers in the correct places

Track 11

J'ai un petit chaton
I have a little kitten

Il est si mignon
He is so sweet

Il chasse les souris
He chases mice

Petit chaton, où es-tu?
Little kitten, where are you?

Je suis sous le lit
I am under the bed

Sous le lit?
Under the bed?

Sous le lit!
Under the bed!

J'ai un petit chaton

Il est si mignon

Il m'apporte des souris
He brings me mice

Petit chaton, où es-tu?

Je suis sur le lit
I am on the bed

Sur le lit?
On the bed?

Sur le lit!
On the bed!

J'ai un petit chaton

Il est si mignon

Écoute, il ronronne
Listen, he is purring

Petit chaton où es-tu?

Je suis dans le lit
I am in the bed

Shhh, je dors ...
Shhh, I'm sleeping ...

Bonne nuit!
Good night!

Où? 37

MES AFFAIRES

9. My things

Help your child: This unit introduces the idea of possession with the word 'my'. The word for 'my' changes to agree with the noun it is describing (i.e. it becomes masculine, feminine or plural) so it requires some practice. Persevere and you will be surprised how easily your child can adopt grammatical ideas from another language. Why not have your child label his or her possessions in French?

Colle la bonne vignette au bon endroit
Stick the stickers in the correct space

Astuce
Do the ones you can guess first and see what you have left.

le cartable   la trousse   les livres   les cahiers   le cahier de textes

la gomme   le crayon   les feutres   le stylo   la règle

Le détective!
Did you notice?

To make a French word plural (which means if there is more than one of something) you add −s or −x and *le* or *la* becomes *les*.

le livre = the book (one book)
les livres = the books (more than one book)

Remets les lettres en ordre pour trouver ce qu'il y a dans la trousse
Put the letters in order to find out what's in the pencil case

LOTSY ....   NOYARC ....   MEGOM ....

LEGÈR ....   SCIUAXE ....

Le détective!
Did you notice?

The word for 'my' in the unit title 'My things' is *mes*. But you might have noticed earlier on in the book that there are other ways to say 'my'. It depends on the gender and quantity of the thing(s) you're referring to:

	masculine	feminine	plural
the ------>	le	la	les
my ------>	mon	ma	mes

The word for 'my' is:

mon with masculine nouns: *mon père* – my father; *mon stylo* – my pen

ma with feminine nouns: *ma mère* – my mother; *ma veste* – my jacket

mes with plural nouns: *mes parents* – my parents; *mes affaires* – my things

Complète avec *mon*, *ma* ou *mes*
Fill in the gaps with *mon*, *ma* or *mes*

Petit Dico
les ciseaux scissors
le bâton de colle glue

Dans .... cartable j'ai .... livres, ... cahiers, ...

cahier de textes, ... trousse et .... chaussures de foot.

Dans .... trousse j'ai .... stylo, ... crayons, ...

feutres, ... gomme, ... bâton de colle et .... ciseaux.

Mes affaires 39

L'alphabet
The alphabet

Écoute et participe
Listen and join in

Track 12

A comme arbre

B comme banane

C comme caméléon

D comme dragon

E comme escargot

F comme France

G comme girafe

H comme hibou

I comme igloo

J comme judo

K comme kangourou

L comme lapin

M comme main

40 Mes affaires

N comme neige

O comme orange

P comme parapluie

Q comme quatre

R comme radio

S comme souris

T comme télé

U comme uniforme

V comme vélo

W comme wagon

X comme xylophone

Y comme yaourt

Z comme zèbre

Mes affaires 41

De la Tête aux Pieds

10. From head to toe

Help your child: In this unit your child will learn how to describe the different parts of the body. When seeing new words for the first time, encourage your child to use their knowledge of English to look for words that are similar in French.

Relie les noms aux image
Link the names to the picture

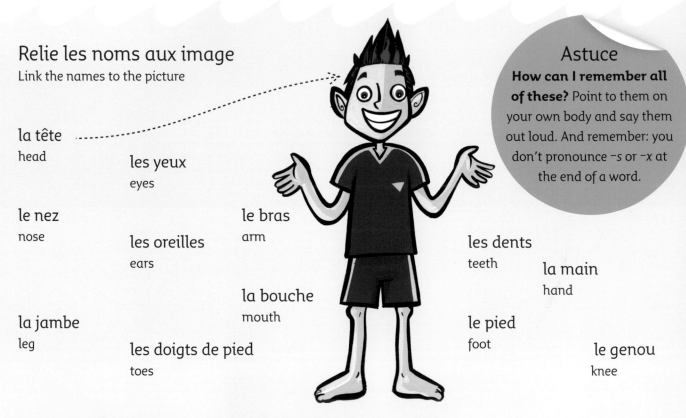

la tête
head

les yeux
eyes

le nez
nose

les oreilles
ears

le bras
arm

la bouche
mouth

les dents
teeth

la main
hand

la jambe
leg

les doigts de pied
toes

le pied
foot

le genou
knee

Astuce
How can I remember all of these? Point to them on your own body and say them out loud. And remember: you don't pronounce −s or −x at the end of a word.

C'est quelle partie du corps?
Which part of the body is it?

C'est ....

C'est ....

C'est ....

C'est ....

C'est ....

C'est ....

Chanson: Écoute et chante
Song: Listen and sing

Track 13

Un kilomètre à pied, ça use, ça use,
One kilometre on foot, it wears, it wears,

Un kilomètre à pied ça use les doigts de pied
One kilometre on foot, it wears out your toes!

Deux kilomètres à pied …

Relie les phrases
Draw in linking lines to join the phrases

J'écoute avec	avec les yeux
Je sens l'odeur	sur mes pieds
Je mange	avec les jambes
Je regarde	les oreilles
Je touche	avec la bouche
Je marche	avec mes doigts
Je mets des gants	sur ma tête
Je mets des chaussettes	avec le nez
Je mets un chapeau	sur mes mains

Avec means 'with' · You wear *gants* to keep warm when building a snowman! · Say the word *odeur* aloud to help you guess what it means · Say the words *marche* and *touche*. What English words do they sound like? · A 'manger' is where you put food for animals.

Astuce
Do the ones you can and then see what you have left.

Mots cachés: Combien de parties du corps peux-tu trouver?
Word search: How many parts of the body can you find?

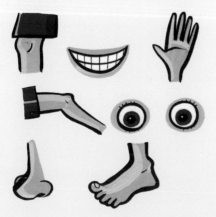

m	v	y	c	j	a	m	b	e
n	a	b	o	u	c	h	e	d
e	p	i	e	d	y	e	u	x
z	g	e	n	o	u	a	l	u

De la tête aux pieds 43

Mon anniversaire
My birthday

C'est quand ton anniversaire?
When is your birthday?

Mon anniversaire est le 15 juillet
My birthday is on the 15th July

La date
le premier 1st
deux 2 ...

onze 11
douze 12
treize 13
quatorze 14
quinze 15
seize 16
dix-sept 17
dix-huit 18
dix-neuf 19
vingt 20
vingt-et-un 21
vingt-deux 22 ...

vingt-neuf 29

trente 30
trente-et-un 31

Le mois
janvier – January
février – February
mars – March
avril – April
mai – May
juin – June
juillet – July
août – August
septembre – September
octobre – October
novembre – November
décembre – December

Astuce
How do you say fifteen<u>th</u>?
Well, in French you don't need to! They just say 'my birthday is the fifteen July'. Simple! Except if your birthday is on the 1st – that's *le premier*!

C'est quand ton anniversaire?

Mon anniversaire est le ....

44 **De la tête aux pieds**

Résumé

Summary

Choisis un mot de la case pour compléter les phrases

Choose a word from the box to complete the sentences

un   masculine   le   une

la   feminine   mes

equally

les   end   ma

differently

mon   les

1. I know that in French all nouns are either .... or ....

2. The word for 'the' is .... or ....

3. The word for 'a' is .... or ....

4. A lot of words are related to English words but are pronounced ....

5. In French you stress each part of the word ....

6. You do not pronounce −s or −t at the .... of a word.

7. The word for 'the' with a plural word is .... as in .... yeux.

8. The word for 'my' is .... , ... or ....

Answer key

Pg 4
le crocodile
le kangourou
le lion
l'hippopotame
la girafe
le tigre
l'éléphant

Which is true?:
2. *ch* sounds like *sh* in shoe

Pg 5
Word search
tigre
lion
girafe
éléphant
kangourou
tortue
crocodile

Which is true?
2. *é* sounds like *ay* in day

Pg 7
7 = sept
2 = deux
6 = six
10 = dix
5 = cinq
3 = trois

Which is true?
1. B
2. A
3. C
4. A
5. C
6. B
7. B

Pg 8
huit os (8)
deux os (2)
sept os (7)
quatre os (4)
trois os (3)
neuf os (9)

chien chenille cinq chat
deux dessin disque dix
singe sept souris six
question queue quatre qui
fruit huit nuit bruit
trois bois fois mois

Pg 11
Clara = red & yellow
Thomas = blue & green
Hugo = black & white
Stéphanie = pink & grey
Zoé = blue & yellow
Louis = green & red

Pg 12
une souris grise
une chenille verte

Pg 14
Sophie: black hair and
  brown eyes
Marc: brown hair and
  green eyes
Marie: blue eyes and
  brown hair
Philippe: black hair and
  brown eyes
Richard: red hair and
  hazel eyes
Nadine: blonde hair and
  blue eyes

Pg 15
1. Zoé
2. Clara
3. Thomas
4. Hugo
5. Louis
6. Stéphanie

Pg 20
le bateau
le chapeau
l'oiseau
le soleil
la feuille
la maison
la pomme
l'escargot
l'arbre
l'écureuil
le château
l'hélicoptère
l'hôtel
l'hippopotame
l'école

Pg 26
un parapluie
une fleur
un clown
une veste
une chaussure
un chapeau
une cravate
une chemise

Pg 27
Le clown porte, un
  pantalon, une veste
  une chemise, une cravate,
  un chapeau, une fleur,
  un parapluie et deux
  enormes chaussures.

Pg 28
une robe rose
  = a pink dress
un jean bleu
  = blue jeans
un tee-shirt jaune
  = a yellow T-shirt
un pantalon gris
  = grey trousers
une chemise bleue
  = a blue shirt

un sweat vert
  = a green sweatshirt
un jogging bleu
  = a blue tracksuit
un short rouge
  = red shorts
un maillot de bain rouge
  = a red swimming
  costume
un pyjama bleu
  = blue pyjamas
un maillot de foot orange
  = an orange football shirt
une jupe noir
  = a black skirt

Pg 29
des baskets rouges
  = red trainers
des chaussures noirs
  = black shoes
des tennis blancs
  = white tennis shoes
des pantoufles roses
  = pink slippers
des bottes marron
  = brown boots
des palmes jaunes
  = yellow flippers
des bottes de caoutchou
  violets = red wellies

je joue au basket = trainers
je vais à l'école = school
  shoes
il pleut = wellies
il neige = snow boots
je vais au lit = slippers
je vais faire de la plongée
  = flippers

Pg 31
des baskets = trainers
une chemise = shirt
un jean = jeans
un jogging = tracksuit
une jupe = skirt
un maillot de foot
  = football shirt
un maillot de bain
  = swimming costume
un pantalon = trousers
un pyjama = pyjamas
une robe = dress
un short = shorts
un sweat = sweatshirt
un tee-shirt = T-shirt

Pg 32
1. samedi
2. jeudi
3. mercredi
4. mardi
5. dimanche
6. lundi
7. vendredi
The word that is spelled
  out is 'semaine'

Pg 34
Je me cache sous la table
Je saute sur le trampoline
Je dors dans mon lit

Pg 36
La souris est ...
sur le chapeau
sous le chapeau
dans le chapeau

Le gâteau est ...
sur la table
sous la table
dans l'estomac du chien!

Pg 38
le cartable = schoolbag
la trousse = pencil case
les livres = books
les cahiers = notebooks
le cahier de textes =
  homework diary
la gomme = rubber
le crayon = pencil
les feutres = felt-tipped
  pens
le stylo = pen
la règle = ruler

LOTSY = stylo
NOYARC = crayon
MEGOM = gomme
LEGÈR = règle
SCIUAXE = ciseaux

Pg 39
Dans mon cartable j'ai mes
  livres, mes cahiers, mon
  cahier de textes, ma
  trousse et mes
  chaussures de foot.

Dans ma trousse j'ai mon
  stylo, mes crayons, mes
  feutres, ma gomme,
  mon bâton de colle et
  mes ciseaux.

Pg 42
1. C'est la bouche
2. C'est le nez
3. C'est les yeux
4. C'est la jambe
5. C'est le bras
6. C'est le pied

Pg 43
j'écoute avec les oreilles
je sens l'odeur avec le nez
je mange avec la bouche
je regarde avec les yeux
je touche avec mes doigts
je marche avec les jambes
je mets des gants sur mes
  mains
je mets des chaussettes
  sur mes pieds

je mets un chapeau sur
  ma tête

Word search
jambe
oreilles
main
bouche
genou
nez
pied
yeux

Résumé
1. masculine, feminine
2. le, la
3. un, une
4. differently
5. equally
6. end
7. les, les
8. mon, ma, mes

46